When did dinosaurs live?

The first dinosaurs lived about 240 million years ago, long before there were people. Dinosaurs evolved from other animals called dinosauromorphs. They were cat-sized reptiles.

I'm a dinosauromorph. When an animal evolves it changes over time, so it can survive in a changing world.

I'm one of the first dinosaurs. I lived about 230 million years ago.

Herrerasaurus

Tarbosaurus

I'm one of the last dinosaurs. I roamed the planet 70 million years ago.

Were all dinosaurs huge?

Dinosaurs came in all shapes and sizes. The largest ones were called titanosaurs. They were more than 20 metres long and weighed as much as six elephants!

Argentinosaurus

I'm one of the biggest dinosaurs ever. Can you guess where in the world I came from?

This tiny terror is Microraptor. It is just 40–60 centimetres long

Being small helps me to glide from trees.

Where did they live?

The first dinosaurs lived on Pangaea – a single, giant slab of land. The world was very hot and dry and there was just one ocean called Panthalassa. Dinosaurs could walk all the way from the North Pole to the South Pole. We call this time in Earth's history the Triassic.

PANGAEA

Who would be at a dino party?

Dinosaurs were reptiles, so they might invite other reptiles. These baby *Maiasaura* have just hatched, so they are sharing their birthday party. Can you spot which guests are not dinosaurs?

Maiasaura

Who looked after the babies?

Maiasaura mums took good care of their nests, eggs and young. They protected them from hungry *Troodon*.

Watch out kids, that hungry Troodon has its big eyes on you!

Troodon was an intelligent dinosaur with big eyes and sharp claws

Why do dinos have such strange names?

Dinosaur names are often made up of more than one word. Put together, the words tell us more about the dinosaur.

Carcharodontosaurus shark-tooth-lizard

Tyrannosaurus rex tyrant-lizard-king

Guanlong crown-dragon

Maiasaura good mother-lizard

Triceratops three-horned-face

Torosaurus bull-lizard

Mei long sleeping-dragon

Hey, who is Tyrannosaurus rex?

Mei long was covered in bird-like feathers and may have been very colourful

Did dinosaurs have fur?

No, dinosaurs didn't have fur but many of them had feathers. The feathers were often fluffy, but some dinosaurs grew long feathers, like modern birds. Fuzzy, fluffy feathers kept dinosaurs warm.

Yutyrannus was up to 9 metres long and covered in fuzzy feathers

Did you know?

A fully-grown *T rex* was **longer** and **heavier** than a bus and its skull was so heavy you'd need a forklift truck to pick it up.

In 1824 **Megalosaurus** was the first dinosaur to be named. When its thighbone was dug up people thought it belonged to a human giant!

Meat-eating dinosaurs had long, curved, sharp teeth.

Titanosaurs were huge, long-necked dinosaurs but they were not the largest animals to ever live. The **blue whale**, which lives in our oceans today, wins that prize.

Plant-eaters had peg-like or spoon-shaped teeth.

All dinos could **walk**, some of them could **swim** and others – like *Microraptor* – could **glide** between trees.

Dinosaurs didn't have **kneecaps**, but no one knows why!

T rex and *Tarbosaurus* might have made good **ballet dancers** – they balanced beautifully on their tiptoes!

Ichthyosaurs were fast-swimming reptiles that lived in the sea. They looked like whales or dolphins, but were related to **snakes** and **lizards**.

Which dinosaurs had the longest necks?

Sauropods were a group of huge dinosaurs with very long necks, like *Brachiosaurus*. Having a long neck meant that sauropods could reach high up into trees to eat leaves. They might spend all day eating.

Mamenchisaurus had a long, thin neck that was 12 metres in length

Mamenchisaurus

Brachiosaurus

Parasaurolophus

Could dinosaurs roaaarr?

No one knows what sounds dinosaurs made. They may have roared, growled, chirped, tweeted – or made no sounds at all. *Parasaurolophus* had a long, hollow crest on its head. It may have blown air through the crest to make honking sounds – like a trumpet!

Diplodocus

Diplodocus had a long, bendy tail too, which it used to wallop other dinosaurs

Do you think I'm handsome?

Oviraptor

Some dinosaurs liked to look good! Horns, frills, head plates and colourful feathers or skin may have all helped male dinosaurs look attractive to female ones.

Who was king of the dinosaurs?

Look out! Here comes *Tyrannosaurus rex* – king of the dinosaurs. *T rex* was a massive 13 metres long and weighed about 7 tonnes – that makes it one of the biggest meat-eaters that's ever lived on land, in the whole history of the planet!

T rex may have hunted in groups. A pack of them would have been a terrifying sight for a Triceratops like me!

Yikes!

Sharp claws on hands and feet

How scary was a T rex?

T rex was one of the scariest dinosaurs to ever live. It was a huge, fearsome, powerful hunter that preyed on other big dinosaurs. It could bite its prey so hard it snapped bones.

When did T rex live?

T rex lived at the end of the Cretaceous Period, 68 to 66 million years ago. Scientists have so far found about 50 skeletons of T rex in North America.

Thick, scaly skin with fuzzy feathers sticking out between the scales

Why are my hands so tiny?

Each eyeball was the size of a grapefruit

T rex had small arms and hands but they were very strong, and had nasty claws. T rex may have gripped prey close to its chest as it sank its razor-sharp teeth into the flesh.

Great sense of smell, and good eyesight

Huge jaws were packed with long, razor-sharp teeth

How many?

3

The number of claws *Therizinosaurus* had on each hand – the longest was 71 centimetres long! It probably used its claws to grab branches and pull leaves to its mouth.

10

The size in centimetres of the smallest known dinosaur eggs. The biggest were 30 centimetres long – twice as big as an ostrich egg.

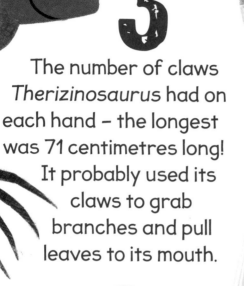

50

The number of new species of dinosaur being discovered every year.

In 1905 the bones of a *T rex* were put on display in a museum for the first time. Scientists thought they were just **8 million** years old!

T rex could run at speeds of about **30** kilometres an hour – that's faster than an elephant but much slower than a racehorse.

Most dinos probably grew quickly and died before they reached the age of **30**.

The world was about **6°C** hotter during the Cretaceous than it is today. The hot, steamy weather meant that lush forests could grow as far as the North Pole!

19 The number of bones in the neck of Mamenchisaurus – more than any dinosaur discovered so far.

2 The weight in kilograms that a 10-year-old T rex would have gained every day! A newly hatched T rex would have been the size of pigeon, but it grew super fast.

The Jurassic Period lasted **55 million years**. Then Pangaea began to break up into big chunks of land called continents.

How did dinosaurs defend themselves?

Many plant-eating dinosaurs had bony armour to protect them from attack. Thick slabs of bone, plates, scales, spikes and bony bumps all helped ankylosaurs fend off the razor-sharp claws and dagger-like teeth of meat-eating dinosaurs.

Why is there a big club on your tail?

Smash!

Ankylosaurus

I'm an ankylosaur from the Late Cretaceous. I have a huge club on the end of my tail and it's very useful for walloping anything that attacks me – like that Trex over there!

Trex

Why did Triceratops have horns?

Roar!

i use my long horns to defend myself against Trex and other big predators. i can raise the big bony frill around my neck to make myself look scarier too!

i'm a bonehead dinosaur. My skull is 25 centimetres thick. i can use it to batter my rivals, and it makes me look cool too!

Why is your head so big?

Bonehead dinosaurs used their big heads to ram into each other

Pachycephalosaurus

Crash!

What did dinosaurs eat?

Some dinosaurs hunted animals to eat, other dinosaurs ate plants, and some ate whatever they could find!

I'm fully armed with slashing, gripping claws and jaws lined with razor-sharp teeth. I'm fast, smart... and hungry for meat!

Raptors, like Deinonychus, were light on their feet and super speedy

Sauropelta

I eat plants. My body is covered in bony plates and spikes that make it difficult for Deinonychus to attack me!

How much did T rex eat?

Yum!

T rex was a hungry beast that needed about 110 kilograms of meat a day. That's more than 1000 burgers!

Plant-eaters like me graze on low-growing plants and leaves. Even our teeth are shaped like leaves!

I look like an ostrich with my long legs, feathers and toothless beak. I mostly peck at bugs, lizards and other small animals.

Deinonychus

Ornithomimus

How fast could a dinosaur run?

Plant-eating dinosaurs were slow movers, but most predator dinosaurs needed speed to hunt and catch their prey.

Ornithomimus was one of the fastest dinosaurs, with top speeds of 35 kilometres an hour or more

Could dinosaurs fly?

Yes, and they still do! Flying dinosaurs are all around us. We call them birds.

Over a long time, some dinosaurs began to develop bird-like bodies with wings and feathers. By 150 million years ago, the first birds had appeared. That means all birds are actually dinosaurs!

What was the first bird called?

Archaeopteryx — that's me! I have teeth, claws on my wings and a long, bony tail. I can climb, run, glide and even fly a little.

I lived 130 million years ago. I could glide between trees and flap my wings.

Microraptor

Quetzalcoatlus

I'm a giant pterosaur. I have a wingspan of 12 metres and I'm one of the biggest animals to ever fly – one of my feet is bigger than a human's leg!

What is a pterosaur?

Pterosaurs were flying reptiles that lived at the same time as the dinosaurs. Their wings were made of thin skin, spread out between the bones in their arms and fingers, and they were superb flyers.

Would you rather?

Have a **Maiasaura** or **Majungatholus** for a mum? Scientists think that Majungatholus may have eaten members of its own family!

Fight a T rex or **fly** with a pterosaur?

Be a **fast-running** Gallimimus or a **slow-moving** Stegosaurus?

Have **teeth** like T rex or a **neck** like Supersaurus? You'd either need a very big toothbrush, or a very long scarf!

If you had the body of a sauropod would you use your long tail to **splash** in water, or let people **slide** down it?

Be as **big** as Brachiosaurus or as **small** as Microraptor?

Be covered in a coat of **soft, fluffy feathers** or have **scary horns** growing on your face?

Have tea with a *Tarbosaurus*, **cuddle** a *Carcharodontosaurus* or **stroke** a *Stegosaurus*?

23

How could sauropods grow so big?

Sauropods were giant plant-eaters. They had big bones and huge muscles to move their bodies. They also had holes and air sacs in their bones, which kept them light. Without these, sauropods would have been even heavier!

Could a dinosaur crush a car?

Argentinosaurus weighed over 60 tonnes. If it sat on a car, it could crush it in an instant! *T rex* had one of the most powerful bites of any animal ever known. It could have crushed a car in its mighty jaws!

Crunch!

Brachiosaurus

I am three times taller than a giraffe!

How did dinosaurs kill their prey?

They were equipped with some lethal weapons! Claws, jaws, teeth and tails could all be used to injure, catch or kill other animals. Raptors had long, curved claws on their feet for slashing and slicing.

What happened to the dinosaurs?

After more than 150 million years of ruling the world, disaster struck the dinosaurs. An enormous space rock, called an asteroid, smashed into Earth.

How did Earth change?

It turned cold and dark, and there was very little food because plants couldn't grow. Over the next few thousand years, most types of animals, including the dinosaurs, went extinct.

The dinosaurs began to die, along with many other animals

The asteroid hit Earth with the explosive force of a billion giant bombs

There were giant waves, floods and burning winds before dark clouds of dust filled the sky

Are the dinosaurs still alive?

Yes they are! Birds belong to the dinosaur family, and some survived the asteroid, along with other animals. Today, more than 10,000 different types of bird live all over the world.

Eagles have sharp claws and beaks like many dinosaurs did

Can you believe I'm a dinosaur? RAAA!

Huge, flightless terror birds lived in South America about two million years ago

Ducks, geese and chickens are dinosaur relatives

Who collects dino poo?

① This dinosaur died and its soft parts rotted away

We do! We're palaeontologists (say: pal-ee-on-tol-oh-jists). We look for the remains of animals that lived long ago.

What's a fossil?

A fossil is the remains of an animal that has turned to stone over millions of years.

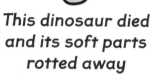

② Its bones were covered in sand or mud

We look at fossils of bones and footprints. Fossil poo helps us to work out what dinosaurs ate.

Where can I find dinosaurs?

Lots of museums have dinosaur fossils you can look at. They are being dug up all over the world, from the USA to China! Mudstone, sandstone and limestone are all good rocks in which to find fossils.

Whose tooth is that?

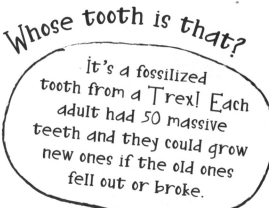

It's a fossilized tooth from a Trex! Each adult had 50 massive teeth and they could grow new ones if the old ones fell out or broke.

③ Over time, the bones were buried by more sand or mud and turned to stone – they have been fossilized

My bones are revealed when land erodes (wears away).

A compendium of questions

What was the biggest scary dinosaur to ever live?

It may have been the super scary *Spinosaurus*. It was probably longer and heavier than *T rex*, and its huge head had crocodile-like jaws lined with teeth.

How many types of dinosaur are there?

About 2000 types have been found and named so far, but there are plenty more to discover.

Why did Brachiosaurus eat stones?

Like many reptiles, *Brachiosaurus* probably swallowed stones to help grind up tough plant food in its stomach.

Were dinosaurs clever?

Some were! *Troodon* had a big brain for its size. It was smarter than a turtle but not as clever as a parrot.